A T
Central NY

Authentic Italian family recipes handed down from generation to generation unique to the area of Utica, New York

Researched, Compiled and Written
by
James P. Malagese

This book is dedicated to my family.
Cooking has always been a big part of their lives
and has made its way into mine. The recipes
included in this book have been taken mainly from
little pieces of aged paper, hand
written in barely legible cursive and stuffed
together in cookbooks older than me.

I'd like to especially thank my mother
Marianne Malagese, my aunt Diane Angelino
and my cousin Francine Talerico from whom
I received most of these family recipes.

I hope you enjoy cooking from this book as much
as I enjoyed writing it.

Mangiare!

Table of Contents

Appetizers *(antipasti)*   **5**

Soups & Stews *(minestre)*   **21**

Salads *(insalate)*   **29**

Sides *(lati)*   **35**

Pasta & Sauces *(pasta e salse)*   **47**

Land and Sea *(terra e mare)*   **67**

Desserts *(dolce)*   **79**

Your Personal Recipes   **99**

Appetizers
(antipasti)

Bruschetta

1 loaf French Bread
2 - 3 cloves Fresh Garlic (peeled and kept whole)
Extra Virgin Olive Oil
Salt

1. Slice bread on the bias into half inch pieces.
2. On a hot grill, toast slices brown on both sides.
3. Immediately after taken off the grill, generously rub one side of toasted bread with garlic cloves.
4. Lay out on a baking sheet, drizzle with olive oil and sprinkle with salt.

This recipe is the classic recipe and can be used as a base.

Bruschetta Toppings

Tomato-Basil

- Dice up some ripe Roma Tomatoes, White Onions and Fresh Basil
- Mix together with Extra Virgin Olive Oil
- Romano Cheese, Salt & Pepper to taste

Three Cheese

- Grate equal amounts of Mozzarella, Provolone and Swiss Cheese
- Mix together and generously top each Bruschetta
- Broil until melted and slightly brown

Crab Sauté

- In a medium skillet, sauté finely chopped celery, onions, red bell peppers and garlic until tender
- Add lump crabmeat and a pinch of cayenne pepper
- Salt & Pepper to taste

Vegetarian

- Dice up some of your favorite vegetables
- Add roasted garlic, salt & pepper and mix
- After spooning mix on each Bruschetta, top each piece with Fresh Mozzarella Cheese
- Warm in oven until cheese is slightly melted, but not runny

Tomato Pie

6 cups Flour
1 package Dry Yeast
1 ¾ cups Water
1-12 oz. can Crushed Tomatoes
4 ounces Fresh Basil (chopped)
1 tsp Dry Oregano
2 cloves Garlic (sliced in halves)
½ cup Pecorino Romano Cheese
Vegetable Oil
Garlic Salt

1. Mix flour and 2 teaspoons of salt together in a bowl. Dissolve yeast in 1 cup of warm water and add to flour mix. Add remaining water and knead dough for about 20 minutes. Add extra flour while kneading if sticky. Place in an oiled bowl and cover with dry towel. Set aside in a warm place and let rise.
2. Prepare rectangular no-stick backing sheet by spreading a light coating of vegetable oil.
3. Once dough has doubled in size, knead for another 10 minutes and spread onto baking sheet. Set aside and cover with towel to rise again.
4. In a small pot, combine crushed tomatoes, garlic cloves, basil, and a pinch of black pepper. Cook on medium low heat for one hour.
5. When sauce in ready, remove it from heat and spread entire pot evenly over dough.
6. Evenly spread Romano cheese over sauce and lightly sprinkle oregano and garlic salt over entire pie.

Cook in a preheated oven at 375 ºF for 30 minutes.

White Pie (Garlic Pizza)

6 cups Flour
1 package Dry Yeast
1 ¾ cups Water
4 Fresh Roma Tomatoes (sliced thin)
4 ounces Fresh Basil (chopped large)
1 tsp Dry Oregano
6 cloves Garlic (minced fine)
1 ball Fresh Mozzarella Cheese (sliced thin)
½ cup Pecorino Romano Cheese
½ pound Ricotta Cheese (optional)
Vegetable Oil
Olive Oil

1. Mix flour and 2 teaspoons of salt together in a bowl. Dissolve yeast in 1 cup of warm water and add to flour mix. Add remaining water and knead dough for about 20 minutes. Add extra flour while kneading if sticky. Place in an oiled bowl and cover with dry towel. Set aside in a warm place and let rise.
2. Prepare rectangular no-stick backing sheet by spreading a light coating of vegetable oil.
3. Once dough has doubled in size, knead for another 10 minutes and spread onto baking sheet. Set aside and cover with towel to rise again.
4. When dough has risen again, spread a light layer of olive oil over dough then evenly spread minced garlic.
5. Lay out sliced tomatoes evenly over entire surface followed by fresh basil and mozzarella.
(If you use ricotta you can drop small pieces throughout surface at this step)
6. Sprinkle Romano cheese and oregano over top.

Cook in a preheated oven at 375 °F for 30 minutes.

Sausage Roll

1 pound Pizza Dough (see Tomato Pie, Steps 1-3)
1 pound Bulk Italian Sausage (hot or mild, cooked)
1 Large Egg (beaten)
8 ounces Mozzarella (shredded)
¼ cup Pecorino Romano Cheese

OPTIONAL
Chopped Mushrooms
Diced Cherry Peppers

1. Cook bulk sausage in skillet thoroughly breaking it apart into small pieces with spatula. Drain drippings into small dish and set aside.
2. Roll dough out into a rectangular shape about 1/8 inch thick.
3. In a bowl combine drained sausage meat, cheeses and egg (mushrooms and peppers if desired).
4. Spread mixture over entire dough surface evenly.
5. Carefully roll the dough, jelly roll fashion, placing seam on bottom of a greased cookie sheet.
6. With pastry brush, lightly coat top of roll with sausage drippings.
7. Bake at 375º F for about 20 minutes or until roll is crusty and brown.

Garlic Knots

1 pound Pizza Dough (see Tomato Pie, Steps 1-3)
Frying Oil
Extra Virgin Olive Oil
Garlic Salt
Crushed Red Pepper Flakes

1. Roll dough out into long half inch ropes.
2. Cut each rope into 4 inch segments.
3. Take each segment and tie it in a knot.
4. In a deep fryer or deep skillet, fry each dough knot for about a minute until lightly brown and cooked through.
5. Remove dough from oil and shake excess oil off in a colander.
6. Place dough knots in a large bowl. You may have to do this in groups depending on how many you make and the size of your bowl.
7. Drizzle olive oil over knots, shaking and tossing them in the bowl.
8. Sprinkle garlic salt over knots, shaking and tossing them in the bowl.
9. Sprinkle red pepper flakes over knots, shaking and tossing them in the bowl.

Serve either hot or room temperature. Best if eaten the same day you make them.

VARIATION

Try using infused olive oil to give the knots a different flavor (rosemary, basil, thyme)

Rice Balls

6 cups Cooked Sticky Rice
½ cup Chopped Fresh Flat Leaf Parsely
1 pound Mozzarella (grated)
1 cup Pecorino Romano Cheese
4 Large Eggs
Frying Oil
Salt & Pepper
Plain Breadcrumbs

1. Mix rice, parsley, mozzarella, Romano cheese and eggs thoroughly by hand as you would when making meatballs. Salt and pepper to taste.
2. Roll into meatball size and coat with breadcrumbs.
3. Fry in oil until brown

VARIATIONS

- Stuff a cube of mozzarella in the center of rice ball before coating with breadcrumbs instead of grating.
- Take a few meatballs in sauce, smash them and stuff rice balls with a teaspoon of the smashed meatball before coating with breadcrumbs.
- If you have any Utica Greens left over, stuff the rice balls with a teaspoon of the greens before coating with breadcrumbs.

Sausage Balls

---

1 pound Bulk Italian Sausage (hot or mild)
8 oz block Extra Sharp Cheddar Cheese (grated)
1 cup Bisquick® Biscuit Mix
1 tbsp Water

1. Mix together sausage, cheese and Bisquick® with hands like mixing meatballs.
2. Add water and mix until slightly moist and workable.
3. Roll mix into quarter-sized balls and place on an ungreased cookie sheet about 1 inch apart.
4. Bake at 350°F for 20 minutes.
5. Place balls in a bowl with a couple napkins at the bottom to catch grease drippings.

Eat warm or room temperature.

VARIATIONS

- For a slightly sweeter result, use a pancake mix instead of Bisquick® Biscuit Mix
- Try changing up the type of cheese you use for different varieties.
- Replacing the Italian Sausage with bulk Pork Sausage or Whole Hog Sausage for a tasty breakfast side dish.

Clams Casino

2 dozen Little Neck Clams
2 tsp Olive Oil
2 tsp Butter
½ cup Onions (finely chopped)
¼ cup Green Bell Pepper (finely chopped)
2 cloves Fresh Garlic (minced)
½ tsp Oregano
2 tbsp Pecorino Romano Cheese (finely grated)
4 slices Bacon
1 cup Plain Bread Crumbs
Fresh Chopped Flat Leaf Parsley

1. Shuck clams, separating clam from shell. Chop clams and set aside separately.
2. In a skillet sauté onions and peppers in oil and butter.
3. Add garlic, oregano, cheese and bread crumbs and continue sautéing for another minute.
4. Remove mixture from heat and mix in chopped clams.
5. Spoon mixture into empty clam shells, over stuffing each shell a bit.
6. Cut raw bacon into small 1 inch strips and top each stuffed clam with a strip.
7. Sprinkle parsley over clams and bake in oven at 350°F for about 10 minutes or until bacon is cooked and crisp.

VARIATIONS

Instead of clams, try using mussels or oysters. Due to the size of oysters you may have to double all ingredients.

Crab Stuffed Mushrooms

2 dozen Large Button Mushrooms (stemmed and cleaned)
½ stick Butter
1 Medium Onion (finely chopped)
1 Red Bell Pepper (gutted and finely chopped)
1 stalk Celery (finely chopped)
1 clove Fresh Garlic (minced)
½ tsp Ground Cayenne Pepper
½ tsp Ground Black Pepper
½ tsp Salt (add more to taste if needed)
¼ cup Fresh Chopped Flat Leaf Parsley
½ cup White Wine or Sherry
½ pound Jumbo Lump Crabmeat
½ cup Japanese Bread Crumbs or Plain Bread Crumbs
Grated Pecorino Romano Cheese

1. In a medium sauce pot melt butter and sauté celery, onion, bell pepper and garlic until vegetables are tender.
2. Finely chop mushroom stems and add them to pot. Sauté another minute.
3. Add cayenne pepper, black pepper, salt, and parsley. Stir in and cook for another minute.
4. Add crabmeat and mix well with sautéed vegetables. Continue cooking for an additional 2 to 3 minutes.
5. Add white wine or sherry and continue until alcohol has cooked out of mix (about 5 minutes).
6. Mix in bread crumbs until stuffing is firm and workable. Add more bread crumbs if needed to stiffen.
7. Overstuff each mushroom cap, place in a baking dish side by side so the mushrooms do not fall over. Sprinkle Romano cheese over tops and bake at 350°F for 20 to 25 minutes or until stuffing looks golden brown and mushrooms feel tender.

Sausage Stuffed Mushrooms

2 dozen Large Button Mushrooms (stemmed and cleaned)
½ pound Bulk Italian Sausage (hot or mild)
1 clove Fresh Garlic (minced)
1 clove Shallot (minced)
¼ cup Fresh Chopped Flat Leaf Parsley
½ cup Red Wine
½ cup Japanese Bread Crumbs or Plain Bread Crumbs
2 slices Provolone Cheese (cut into 1 inch strips)
Marinara Sauce

1. Cook sausage loosely breaking it apart with your spatula while cooking.
2. Add garlic, shallots and chopped mushroom stems, continue cooking another 5 minutes.
3. Add red wine and continue until alcohol has cooked out of mix (about 5 minutes).
4. Last mix in bread crumbs until stuffing is firm and workable. Add more bread crumbs if needed to stiffen.
5. Overstuff each mushroom cap, place in a baking dish side by side so the mushrooms do not fall over.
6. Bake at 350°F for 30 minutes or until stuffing looks golden brown and mushrooms feel tender.
7. Top each mushroom cap while hot with a criss-cross of provolone cheese strips.

Top with marinara sauce when serving.

Chicken Wings

Although this appetizer is not an Italian recipe, I had to include it because aside from Buffalo, Utica has got some of the best Chicken Wings I have ever tasted. This recipe was given to me by an old friend that owns his own Pizzeria & Wings restaurant in Utica.

WING SAUCE
½ cup FRANK'S® RedHot® Sauce
½ cup Margarine (melted)
¼ tsp Garlic Salt
½ tsp Celery Salt
1 tbsp Worcester Sauce

Add all ingredients into a bowl and whisk thoroughly. This recipe is for a medium sauce. Adjust the ratio of hot sauce and margarine for a milder or hotter sauce.

Fry your chicken wings in a deep fryer until crispy and cooked throughout. Remove wings from fryer and immediately toss into wing sauce. Coat wings evenly and let them sit in the sauce for a couple minutes.

Serve with celery and blue cheese or ranch dressing.

Chianti

Cooking School in Adine

Soups & Stews
(minestre e stufati)

Mimas Chicken Soup

1 - 4 Piece Chicken (breasts and thighs, skin on)
1 large Onion
4 Celery Stalks
10 Carrots
2 Potatoes (peeled)
4 Chicken Bouillon Cubes
1 box Pastine (small soup pasta)
Water
Salt & Pepper to Taste

1. Place chicken in large 5 quart soup pot. Fill pot ¾ with water and cook on medium-high for about a ½ hour.
2. Skim all the "scum" that floats to the top of the pot and dispose.
3. Turn heat down to medium and add bouillon cubes, salt and pepper to taste.
4. Chop celery into small pieces, dice onion, peal and slice carrots and add to pot. You will also add the potatoes in whole. Let this cook for an additional 2 hours.
5. Carefully remove chicken pieces from pot with tongs, placing them on a plate to cool slightly. When cool enough to handle, remove all meat from the bones, cut up slightly and add back into the pot. Throw bones away.
6. At this point the potatoes will be fully cooked. With a large spoon break them into bite-sized pieces in the pot.
7. Cook Pastine al Dante and set aside until ready to serve the soup.

Italian Wedding Soup

Make tiny ½ inch meatballs and add to soup along with medium chopped Escarole.

Venison Stew

3 pounds Venison Meat (medium cubed)
1 pound Italian Sausage (hot or mild, sliced)
2 stalks Celery (chopped)
5 Carrots (peeled and chopped)
6 Potatoes (peeled and cut into large cubes)
1 bag Frozen Peas
1 - 28oz. can Crushed Tomatoes
Olive Oil
Water
Salt and Fresh Ground Pepper to Taste

1. In a large stew pot, brown meat in oil.
2. Add tomatoes. Fill tomato can ¼ full with water, rinse can and add to the pot.
3. Salt and pepper to taste.
4. When stew comes to a boil add vegetables and cook for 3 to 4 hours on simmer, stirring every half hour.

Roman Egg Soup

1 quart Chicken Stock
4 Large Eggs (beaten)
1½ tsp Semolina Flour
1½ tsp Pecorino Romano or Parmesan Cheese (grated)
Salt and Fresh Ground Pepper to Taste

1. Bring chicken stock to a boil
2. Add flour and cheese to egg mixture and very slowly pour into stock while continuously and vigorously whisking soup. Cook another 5 minutes.
3. Add salt and pepper to taste

Minestrone

1¼ cups Red Beans
¼ pound Pancetta (chopped small)
3 tbsp Olive Oil
1 Onion (chopped)
1 clove Garlic (minced)
2 stalks Celery (chopped)
2 Carrots (sliced)
1 Large Potato
¼ cup Frozen Peas
¼ head Green Cabbage (shredded fine)
1 tbsp Fresh Chopped Flat Leaf Parsley
¼ cup Precooked Rice
¼ cup Tomato Paste
Salt and Pepper to Taste
2 quarts Water
Grated Pecorino Romano for Garnish

1. Soak beans overnight until soft.
2. In a large pot sauté pancetta, onions and garlic in olive oil until light brown.
3. Add celery, carrots, potatoes and cabbage. Continue sautéing until cabbage is tender.
4. Add 1 quart water and bring to a boil. Lower heat to a simmer and continue cooking for 1 hour.
5. Add beans, peas and tomato purée and continue simmering for another half hour.
6. Add rice before serving. Top bowls with grated cheese.

Zuppa Toscana

1 - 16 oz. package Italian Sausage (hot or mild)
2 Potatoes (sliced)
¾ cup Onions (chopped)
6 slices Bacon (chopped small)
1½ tsp Fresh Garlic (minced)
2 cups Escarole (washed and cut thin)
2 tbsp Chicken Stock
1 quart Water
¼ cup Heavy Whipping Cream

1. Bake sausage links onto a sheet pan at 350° F for 20 minutes, or until done. Cut links in half lengthwise, then cut at an angle into half inch slices.
2. In a large skillet, sauté onions and bacon on medium heat until onions are translucent.
3. Add garlic and cook for another minute. Add chicken stock, water and potatoes. Simmer for a half hour or until potatoes are cooked.
4. Add sausage, escarole, and cream. Simmer until slightly thick then serve.

Roma Tomato Soup

6 tbsp Olive Oil
4 Carrots (sliced)
1 Onion (sliced)
1 tbsp Fresh Basil (chopped)
3 - 28 oz. cans Whole Peeled Roma Tomatoes
1 quart Chicken Stock
1 pint Heavy Whipping Cream
Salt and Pepper to Taste

1. Sauté vegetables and basil in olive oil until soft.
2. Add tomatoes and chicken stock. Simmer for 20 minutes.
3. Add Heavy cream and stir.
4. Cool slightly then purée in food processor and serve.

Roma

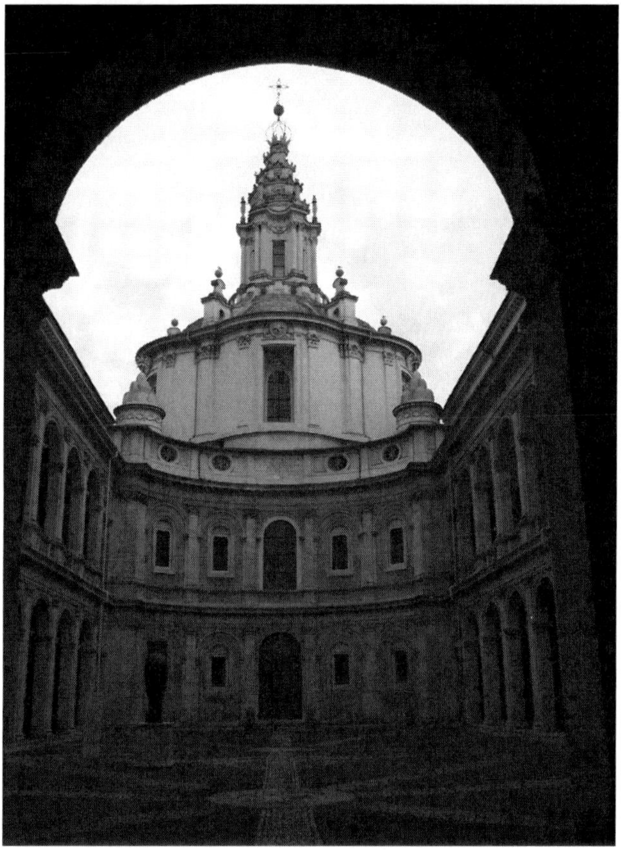

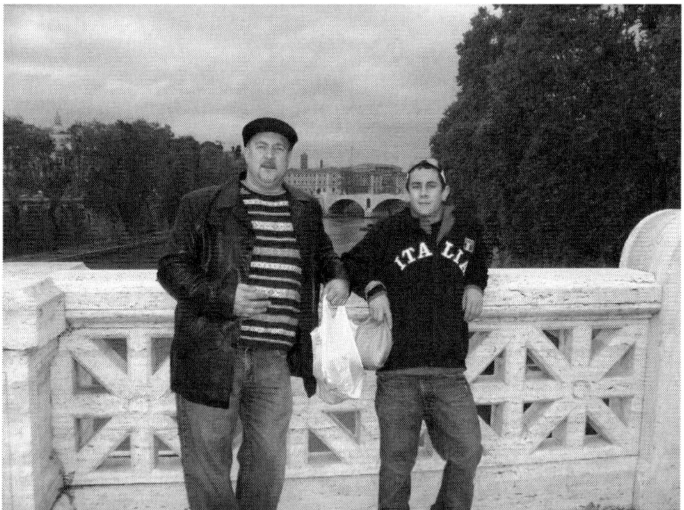
ITALIA

Salads
(insalate)

Antipasto

Ensalata
1 head Iceberg Lettuce
1 can Pitted Black Olives
1 jar Pitted Green Olives
2 Roasted Red Bell Pepper (1 small jar)
4 Fresh Roma Tomatoes (sliced)
1 ball Fresh Mozzarella (sliced)
½ pound Provolone Cheese (cut into cubes)
½ pound Salami (cut into strips)
½ pound Pepperoni (sliced thin)
½ pound Sopressata (cut into strips)
1 can Tuna or 8 oz. Fresh Grilled Tuna (flaked)

Dressing
3 tbsp Extra Virgin Olive Oil
2 tbsp Red Wine Vinegar
1/2 tsp Dried Oregano
1 clove Fresh Garlic (minced fine)
Salt and Pepper to Taste

1. On a large serving platter, spread out lettuce covering entire surface.
2. Arrange all other ingredients to your liking. There is no right or wrong way to do this. Be creative!
3. In a bottle, combine all dressing ingredients and shake vigorously.
4. Evenly pour over salad just before serving.

Ensalata Capresi

4 Large Roma Tomatoes
2 balls Fresh Mozzarella Cheese
8 - 10 Fresh Basil Leaves
Extra Virgin Olive Oil
Balsamic Vinegar
Salt and Fresh Ground Pepper

1. Slice tomatoes and mozzarella to the same thickness.
2. Arrange tomatoes, cheese and basil alternating around a serving dish.
3. Drizzle with olive oil and balsamic vinegar.
4. Sprinkle with salt and fresh ground pepper.

Caponata

4 - 6 small Onions (sliced)
12 Mixed Bell Peppers (green, yellow, red, orange)
2 Eggplant (diced)
1 bunch Celery (chopped)
1 - 28oz. can Whole Peeled Tomatoes
1 small bottle Capers
1 small bottle Green Cocktail Olives
2 cups White Wine Vinegar
2 cups Sugar
Oregano, Garlic Salt & Fresh Ground Pepper to Taste

Dice eggplant, sauté until tender and set aside to cool. Fry peppers and add tomatoes. Let simmer and set aside. Sauté onions with celery and set aside when tender. Mix cooked vegetables with sugar, capers and olives. Add oregano, garlic salt and pepper to taste. Serve in a bowl.

Joey G's Salad

¼ cup Italian "Long Hot" Peppers (sliced)
¼ cup Italian Sweet Peppers (sliced)
¼ cup Sweet Cherry Peppers (sliced)
1 cup Calamata Olives (sliced)
2 cloves Fresh Garlic (minced)
1 can Mushrooms
¼ cup Olive Oil

Toss together and chill before serving.

Roasted Pepper Trio Salad

3 Roasted Red Bell Peppers
2 Roasted Yellow or Orange Bell Peppers
2 Roasted Green Bell Peppers
½ cup Sundried Tomatoes (cut into strips)
1 clove Garlic (minced)
2 tbsp Balsamic Vinegar
5 tbsp Extra Virgin Olive Oil
½ tsp Chili Sauce
4 Canned Artichoke hearts (quartered)
4 Fresh Basil Leaves (chopped)
Salt and Fresh Ground Pepper to Taste

1. Mix olive oil, vinegar, chili sauce, salt and pepper. Set aside until needed.
2. Combine all vegetables, mixing them up thoroughly.
3. Toss together liquid mixture and vegetables.
4. Serve in a large bowl and sprinkle with fresh basil.

Old Fashion Macaroni Salad

1 pound Elbow Macaroni (cooked al Dante)
2 stalks Celery (chopped)
1 Carrot (grated)
6 Hard Boiled Medium Eggs
1 small can Chopped Black Olives
1 small jar Chopped Green Olives
½ - ¾ cup Mayonnaise
Salt & Pepper to Taste
Paprika for Garnish

Mix all ingredients above, only using four chopped hard boiled eggs. Place in large bowl and decorate with the two remaining hard boiled eggs, sliced. Sprinkle top with paprika and parsley.   Chill for several hours before serving.

Old Fashion Potato Salad

5 pounds Boiled Pealed Potatoes
2 stalks Celery (chopped)
1 Whole Dill Pickle (chopped)
6 Hard Boiled Medium Eggs
1 small can Chopped Black Olives
1 small jar Chopped Green Olives
½ - ¾ cup Mayonnaise
Salt & Pepper to Taste
Paprika & Chopped Parsley for Garnish

Mix all ingredients above, only using four chopped hard boiled eggs. Place in large bowl and decorate with the two remaining sliced hard boiled eggs and chopped olives. Sprinkle top with paprika and parsley. Chill for several hours before serving.

Sides
(Iati)

Utica Greens

1 Medium Onion
2 Hot Cherry Peppers
2 slices of Prosciutto
2 heads of Escarole Greens
2 small Potatoes
2 Cloves of Garlic
¼ cup Pecorino Romano Cheese
¼ cup Progresso Italian Bread Crumbs
Olive Oil
Salt & Fresh Ground Pepper

1. Chop onion, cherry peppers, prosciutto and garlic.
2. Peel and boil potatoes until cooked but slightly hard. Cool and dice into small cubes, set aside until needed.
3. Rinse and cut Escarole, discarding the bottom white core. Flash boil and drain thoroughly.
4. In a hot large sauté pan, add olive oil, onion, cherry peppers and garlic. Cook until tender, about 10 minutes.
5. Add prosciutto and escarole. Cook for another 10 minutes, consistently turning greens in pan. Slowly add Romano cheese during this step, adding a little more each time you turn the greens in the pan. Add a pinch of salt & fresh ground pepper to taste.
6. Add potatoes throughout green.
7. Remove sauté pan from heat and add bread crumbs throughout greens tossing continuously.

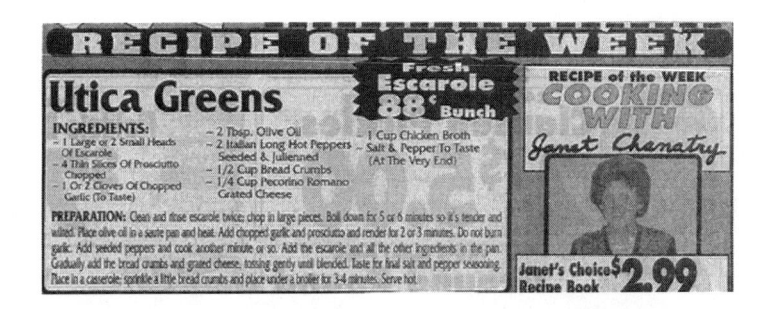

Broccoli di Rabe (Rapini)

1 pound Broccoli Rapini (ends trimmed off)
1 clove Fresh Garlic (sliced thin)
1 cup Chicken Stock
Olive Oil
Pecorino Romano or Parmesan Cheese (grated)

1. Boil broccoli rapini in salted water for about 5 minutes or until tender but not overcooked. Drain well.
2. In a skillet under medium heat, sauté garlic until slightly brown and add rapini. Continue to cook for about 3 to 5 minutes.
3. Add chicken stock and sauté for another 10 to 15 minutes.
4. Pour into serving bowl and top with grated cheese.

Stuffed Artichokes

4 to 6 large Artichokes
¼ cup Pecorino Romano or Parmesan Cheese (grated)
2 Fresh Garlic Cloves (minced)
1½ cups Progresso Italian Seasoned Bread Crumbs
2 tbsp Extra Virgin Olive Oil

1. Cut the bottom stem off of each artichoke along with the pointed tips off of each leaf.
2. Remove any bottom leaves that are not green and wash thoroughly.
3. In a medium bowl, mix cheese, breadcrumbs and olive oil.
4. Working from the bottom up, gently spread the leaves stuffing each layer with the breadcrumb mixture.
5. Place in a baking pan with a half inch of water, cover and bake at 350°F for 45 minutes.

Meatballs

1 pound Ground Beef
4 slices Dry Italian Bread (stale if you have any)
2 cloves fresh Garlic (minced fine)
1 Large Egg
½ cup Pecorino Romano Cheese
¼ cup Parsely Flakes
Salt & Pepper to taste
Frying Oil

1. Mix beef, garlic, eggs, Romano cheese and parsley thoroughly. Add salt and pepper to taste.
2. Soak Italian bread slices in cold water and squeeze dry. Break into small pieces and add to meatball mix.
3. Fry in oil until crispy and done throughout.

Add meatballs to sauce when ready or just eat as is!

VARIATIONS

Substitute different meats for the ground beef. Instead of one pound of beef try a half pound each of pork and veal. Also try equal parts pork, veal and ground beef. For a healthier meatball try substituting ground turkey. One of my favorites is using equal parts ground beef and hot Italian sausage.

Braciole

1 large Round Steak (pounded thin)
½ cup Pecorino Romano Cheese (grated)
1 clove Fresh Garlic (minced fine)
¼ cup Fresh Fresh Flat Leaf Parsely (chopped)
2 Hard Boiled Medium Eggs (sliced)
4 slices Stale Bread (crumbled fine)

1. Pound round steak until thin.
2. Sprinkle bread crumbs over beef surface.
3. Spread garlic over entire surface.
4. Lightly salt and pepper.
5. Cover with Romano cheese and parsley.
6. Spread sliced eggs evenly over entire surface.
7. Drizzle with olive oil.
8. Roll up and tie with white thread.
9. Cut into 3 to 4 inch pieces and fry until brown.
10. Simmer for 1 hour in marinara sauce before serving.

Frittata

> *You can put anything in a Frittata. Vegetables, meats, seafood, herbs...ANYTHING! Try your favorites!!*

6 - 8 Large Eggs
Olive Oil
Salt and Pepper to taste

1. Sauté your selection of vegetables/herbs and or meats/seafood lightly in olive oil seasoned with salt and pepper.
2. Scramble eggs in a bowl and add them into sauté mix.
3. Cook for about 5 minutes or until sides look cooked and puffed.
4. Flip over and continue cooking until frittata is puffed and golden brown.

Rice & Beans

1 Onion (medium chopped)
1 cup Cooked Rice
1 can Pork & Beans
1 clove Fresh Garlic (minced)

1. Sauté onions until translucent.
2. Add garlic and cook for a couple more minutes.
3. Adds rice and beans, heating throughout, and serve.

Pole Beans & Potatoes

1 pound Fresh Pole Beans (cooked)
3 - 4 Potatoes (boiled and cut into cubes)
2 cloves Fresh Garlic (minced)
¼ cup Olive Oil
¼ cup Chopped Fresh Flat Leaf Parsley
¼ cup Romano or Parmesan Cheese (grated)

1. Sauté oil and garlic together until the garlic is light golden brown.
2. Add in beans and potatoes. Toss together cooking for about 5 minutes.
3. Add parsley and cheese. Toss and serve.

Stuffed Melanzane (Eggplant)

6 Eggplants (small)
½ tsp Fresh Basil (chopped)
½ tsp Chopped Fresh Flat Leaf Parsley
¼ cup Olive Oil
2 cups Bread Crumbs (plain)
½ cup Pecorino Romano or Parmesan Cheese (grated)
¼ cup Black Olives (pitted and sliced)
4 Anchovy Fillets (minced into a paste)
1 clove Fresh Garlic (minced)
1 tbsp Capers (well rinsed)
Salt and Pepper to Taste
Marinara Sauce

1. Wash eggplant and cut lengthwise creating two equal halves, leaving the skin on.
2. Scoop out as much of the eggplant as you can without scooping down to the skin. Try leaving between a ¼ inch to a ½ inch.
3. Chop the insides of the eggplant into small pieces and sauté them in olive oil with garlic, basil, parsley, salt and pepper.
4. After eggplant become soft, stir in breadcrumbs, olives, anchovies and capers, Cook another minute.
5. Let cool slightly then start filling the eggplant halves.
6. Top each half with Marinara Sauce and cheese.
7. Bake in a 350° F oven for a half hour or until eggplant bodies are tender.

Minastra

3 cloves Fresh Garlic (minced)
3 Potatoes (peeled, cut and boiled)
2 heads Escarole (washed and chopped)
2 cups Chicken Stock
½ pound Bacon
Olive oil

1. Sauté 2 cloves of garlic in olive oil until golden brown.
2. Add potatoes, escarole and chicken stock. Cook until escarole is tender. Set aside when done.
3. Fry bacon with 1 clove of garlic until bacon is crisp.
4. Pour potatoes & greens into a bowl and pour bacon & garlic over the top.

Pork & Beans

1 Onion (chopped)
1 cup Cooked Rice
1 can Pork & Beans
1 clove Fresh Garlic (minced)
Olive Oil

1. Sauté onions in olive oil until translucent.
2. Add garlic and continue sautéing for another minute.
3. Add rice and beans. Mix thoroughly.
4. Heat through and serve

Stuffed Tomato Provencal

6 Large Tomatoes
4 tbsp Olive Oil
1 Medium Onion (chopped fine)
2 Fresh Garlic Cloves (minced)
¼ cup Fresh Basil Leaves (chopped)
¼ cup Fresh Chives (chopped)
1 tsp Thyme
½ cup Black Olives (pitted and chopped)
½ cup Progresso Italian Bread Crumbs
Pecorino Romano or Parmesan Cheese (grated)
Salt and Pepper To Taste

1. Cut the tops off of each tomato. Scoop out the insides of the tomatoes leaving the thickness of the tomato for a shell. Chop up the tomatoes insides and set aside.
2. In a skillet, sauté onion and garlic in olive oil on medium heat until onions are translucent.
3. Add spices and continue sautéing another minute.
4. Reduce the heat to low and add the tomatoe's chopped insides and black olive. Simmer for 10 to 15 minutes.
5. Stir in bread crumbs and remove from heat.
6. Stuff each tomato generously, top with grated cheese and bake at 350°F for 1 hour or until tomatoes look soft.

Serve hot, cold or even room temperature.

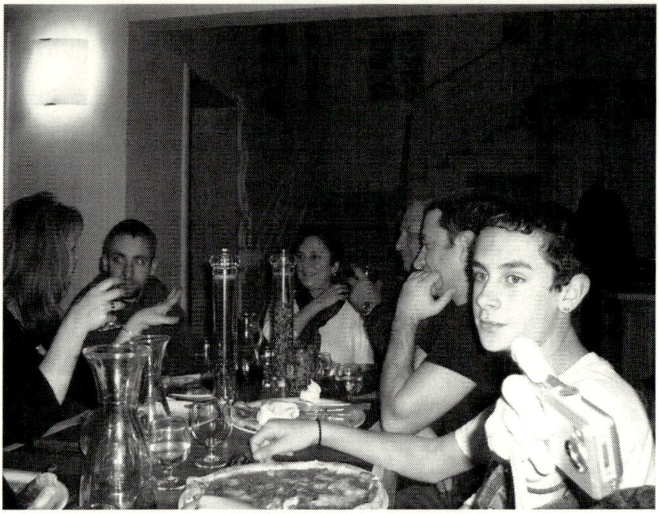

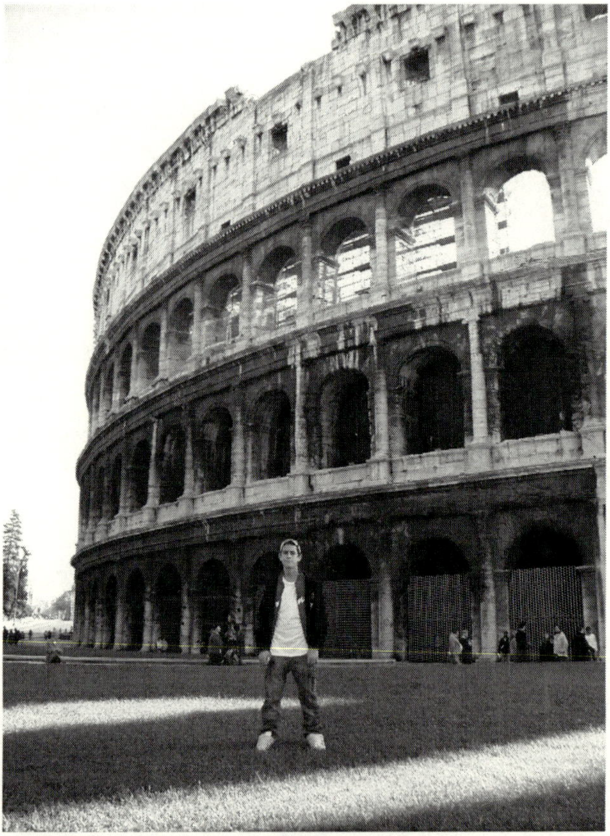

Colosseo

Pasta and Sauces
(pasta e salse)

Gnocchi (potato pasta)

1 pound Waxy Potatoes
2 cups Flour
1 Large Egg
Pinch of Nutmeg

1. Boil potatoes whole leaving skin on until fully cooked. Drain and let slightly cool for about 15 minutes.
2. Peel potatoes while slightly warm, cut and mash adding the egg while mashing.
3. Mix flour and nutmeg in a separate bowl.
4. Place potatoes on a floured surface and slowly add flour to mixture while kneading it into the potatoes.
5. Continue until all flour is used. Add more flour if dough is sticky.
6. Divide dough into 4 equal parts and roll into ¼ - ½ inch ropes. Let sit for 10 to 15 minutes so dough is manageable.
7. Cut dough crosswise into ¾ - 1 inch pieces. Press and roll each gnocchi along the tines of a fork creating a ridged texture. Place pieces on a floured or greased cookie tray and freeze.
8. After pasta is frozen, remove trays from freezer and transfer pasta into freezer bags until ready to use.

VARIATIONS

- Roast a whole garlic bulb and squeeze it into dough for Roasted Garlic Gnocchi.
- Mix chopped cooked spinach and parmesan cheese into dough for Spinach Gnocchi.

Classic Egg Pasta

2 Large Eggs
1 cup Flour
Pinch of Salt

1. Place flour on a clean workable flat surface. Make a well in the center of the flour. Add cracked eggs and salt.
2. With a fork start beating eggs gradually bringing flour from side walls of well into the center. As the center thickens start using your hands until dough is formed. If dough is sticky add a little more flour until manageable. Knead dough for about 10 minutes or until dough is smooth and elastic.
3. At this point your ready to turn the dough into any pasta shape you wish by either rolling it out flat and cutting into noodle strips, running it through a pasta machine, or creating any other shapes you wish to try. You can also use this recipe to make ravioli, tortellini, or any other stuffed pasta dish.

Sunday Sauce

4 - 28 oz. cans Crushed Tomatoes
4 cloves Fresh Garlic (cut in halves)
12 Fresh Basil Leaves (chopped)
4 Large Pork Spare Ribs
1 pound Hot Italian Sausage
2 dozen Meatballs (refer to recipe)
Salt & Pepper to Taste
Olive Oil
Water

1. In a large 8 quart sauce pot add enough olive oil to cover bottom of pot. Heat on medium high until oil becomes hot.
2. Add garlic and ribs and keep in until ribs are brown on all sides, turning them every couple minutes.
3. When ribs are brown, turn the heat down to medium and add tomatoes with a 28oz can of water. Typically we take each empty tomato can and fill it about a quarter way with water, swishing the water around the can getting all of the remaining tomato sauce from the can.
4. When the tomatoes begin heating and start to slightly boil, add Italian sausage links and basil.
Salt and pepper to taste.
5. Lower heat to low or simmer and let cook for at least 2 hours (4 is better).
6. After the second hour of cooking, remove the rib bones. The pork meat should fall off the bones and into the sauce with little help, but help them if they need it.
7. Meatballs should be added about an hour before serving your Sunday Family Dinner.

Serve Family Style with the pasta of your choice.

Bolognaise Sauce (Meat Sauce)

½ pound Ground Beef or Sirloin
½ pound Ground Veal
½ pound Ground Pork
½ pound Bulk Italian Sausage (hot or mild)
1 Carrot (grated)
1 Medium Onion (chopped fine)
1 stalk Celery (chopped fine)
¼ tsp All Spice
¼ tsp Thyme
¼ tsp Basil
¼ cup Parsley
1 - 28oz can Crushed Tomatoes
¼ cup Heavy Cream
¼ cup Red Table Wine

1. Brown all meats in a deep skillet or sauce pan.
2. Drain excess grease and add vegetables.
3. Continue cooking for an additional 10 minutes.
4. Lower heat to medium and add tomatoes, herbs and spices. Continue cooking stirring frequently.
5. When sauce starts to bubble up, lower heat to low and simmer uncovered for about 3 to 4 hours.
6. Add heavy cream and wine 1 hour before serving the sauce over any of your favorite pastas.

Marinara Sauce I

4 - 28 oz. cans Crushed Tomatoes
4 cloves Fresh Garlic (minced)
12 Fresh Basil Leaves (chopped)
Salt & Pepper to Taste
Olive Oil
Water

1. In a large 5 quart sauce pot add enough olive oil to cover bottom of pot. Heat on medium high until oil becomes hot.
2. Add garlic and basil. Sauté until garlic is golden brown.
3. Turn the heat down to medium and add tomatoes. Wash each tomato can out with water adding it to the pot.
4. When the tomatoes begin heating and start to slightly boil, add salt & pepper to taste and simmer for 2 to 4 hours.

Marinara Sauce II

2 - 28oz. Cans Crushed Tomatoes
1 stalk Celery (finely chopped)
1 Carrot (finely chopped)
1 Onion (finely chopped)
2 cloves Fresh Garlic (minced)
½ cup Chopped Fresh Flat Leaf Parsley
2 tsp Olive Oil

1. Sauté chopped vegetables in olive oil until soft.
2. Add garlic and cook for about one minute.
3. Add tomatoes and simmer for 30 minutes.
4. Add parsley and serve or use with your favorite dishes.

Alfredo

½ cup Sweet Unsalted Butter (softened)
1 cup Heavy Cream (room temperature)
1 clove Fresh Garlic (minced)
¾ cup Parmesan Cheese (grated)
¼ tsp Fresh Ground Pepper
1 Large Egg Yolk
Salt to Taste

1. In a sauté pan, melt butter and cook garlic slightly.
2. Add heavy cream and bring it to a medium boil.
3. Add cheese, salt and pepper, stirring constantly so cheese dissolves completely and won't stick to bottom of pan.
4. Mix in egg yolk and continue stirring for another minute.

Toss in your favorite cooked pasta and blend well.

Aioli (Oil & Garlic Sauce)

½ cup Olive Oil
3 cloves Fresh Garlic (minced)
1 tbsp Fresh Fresh Flat Leaf Parsely (chopped)
½ tbsp Crushed Red Pepper
½ cup Water

1. Brown garlic in oil.
2. Add all other ingredients and simmer for about 15 minutes.

Pour over your favorite pasta.

Linguini w/ White Clam Sauce

2 cloves Fresh Garlic
¼ cup Chopped Fresh Flat Leaf Parsley
¼ cup White Wine
2 dozen Fresh Clams
2 tbsp Olive Oil
Linguini
Salt & Pepper to Taste
Pecorino Romano Cheese & Crushed Red Pepper

1. Sauté garlic in olive oil until golden brown.
2. Add wine and clams. Cook clams until open.
3. Add parsley and pour over cooked linguini.
4. Top with Romano cheese and red pepper to taste. Serve family style.

Linguini w/ Red Clam Sauce

2 cloves Fresh Garlic
¼ cup Chopped Fresh Flat Leaf Parsley
1 - 16 ounce can Chopped Tomatoes
¼ cup Red Wine
2 dozen Fresh Clams
2 tbsp Olive Oil
Linguini
Salt & Pepper to Taste
Pecorino Romano Cheese 7 Crushed Red Pepper

1. Sauté garlic in olive oil until golden brown.
2. Add tomatoes, wine and clams. Cook clams until open.
3. Add parsley and pour over cooked linguini.
4. Top with Romano cheese and red pepper to taste. Serve family style.

Pesto

4 ounces Fresh Basil
2 cloves Fresh Garlic
½ cup Pine Nuts
¾ cup Pecorino Romano Cheese
½ - ¾ cup Olive Oil
1 tsp Salt
½ tsp Fresh Ground Pepper

1. In a blender mix together basil, pine nuts, salt, pepper and garlic.
2. Turn blender on a medium speed, then take the center of the blender top off to slowly add olive oil. Slowly drizzle olive oil into mixture until all is used.
3. After the ingredients have been incorporated together, turn the blender on a slower speed, slowly add Romano cheese. After all the cheese has been added you may need to add a bit more olive oil if the pesto looks too thick.

When using the Pesto, toss it together with whatever your serving it on along with a little hot water to help the Pesto spread evenly throughout the dish. This sauce should never be served thick spread over your entrée, but instead mixed throughout coating whatever your serving it on.

STORING IDEA

After you have made your Pesto Sauce, try filling an ice cube try with the mixture, covering it tightly with plastic wrap and freezing it. You can then take out whatever amounts you need when you need it and keep the remaining sauce on hand for whenever you may need it again.

Chicken Riggies

4 boneless Chicken Breasts
1 large Onion
16 ounces Fresh Mushrooms
1 Green Bell Pepper
6 Hot Cherry Peppers
4 cloves Garlic
1 cup Chicken Broth
1 cup Cooking Sherry or White Wine
1 cup Heavy Whipping Cream
1 small can Sliced Black Olives
1 small can Tomato Sauce
½ cup Chopped Fresh Flat Leaf Parsley
1 pound Rigatoni Pasta
Olive Oil
Flour
Salt & Pepper

1. Cut chicken breast into bite-size pieces and dredge in flour. Fry in olive oil until brown. Remove from oil and set aside.
2. Chop onions, peppers and garlic. Slice mushrooms and set aside.
3. In the bottom of a large stock pot sauté onions and peppers in olive oil until tender. Add mushrooms and garlic and continue for another 10 minutes.
4. Add chicken stock and cooked chicken. Once stock starts boiling add cooking sherry. Turn heat down to medium.
5. After about 10 to 15 minutes add parsley, black olives, heavy cream and tomato sauce.
6. Stir and simmer for an additional 1/2 hour stirring frequently.
7. Cook rigatoni before serving.

Toss Rigatoni and sauce mixture in a large pasta serving bowel. Serve family style.

Vodka Penne

1 tbsp Olive Oil
½ Medium Onion (chopped)
1 - 28 oz. can Whole Peeled Tomatoes in Purée
¼ tsp dried oregano
6 - 8 Fresh Basil Leaves (chopped)
1 tsp Salt
½ tsp Fresh Ground Pepper
8 tbsp Unsalted Butter (1 stick)
12 oz. Fresh White Button Mushrooms (quartered)
½ tsp Crushed Red Pepper Flakes
½ cup Vodka
3 cups Heavy Cream
1½ pounds Penne Rigate
¼ cup Parmesan cheese (grated)

1. In a large saucepan sauté onions until golden brown.
2. Crush tomatoes to desired texture and add them, together with the purée, to the saucepan. Stir in the oregano, basil, salt and pepper and simmer 1 hour to concentrate flavors.
3. While the sauce is cooking, heat 4 tablespoons of the butter in a skillet over medium heat. Sauté the mushrooms and hot pepper flakes until the mushrooms are golden.
4. Carefully add the vodka and simmer for 5 minutes to cook off the alcohol.
5. Add the heavy cream and bring to a simmer; pour the cream mixture into the tomato purée; stir to mix. Keep sauce warm while cooking the pasta.
6. In another pot, cook pasta until al denté. Rinse and drain well. Set aside until needed.
7. To finish the dish, melt the remaining 4 tablespoons of butter in pot you boiled your pasta in. Stir in pasta to glaze, then add Parmesan cheese and mix thoroughly. Add sauce, mix and serve family style.

Pasta Fagioli

2 tbsp Olive Oil
2 cloves Fresh Garlic (minced fine)
2 tbsp Fresh Flat Leaf Parsley (chopped)
1-12oz can Beans of Your Choice
1 cup Marinara Sauce
Pasta of Choice

1. Sauté garlic in olive oil until golden brown.
2. Add Marinara Sauce and a little water, continue cooking for another couple minutes.
3. Add beans and parsley. Do not strain juice from can.
4. Boil pasta al Dente.
5. Cook beans thoroughly and toss together with pasta.

St. Joseph's Day Pasta

3 cloves Fresh Garlic (chopped)
3 tbsp Olive Oil
1 can Chic Peas (drained)
½ cup Progresso Italian Bread Crumbs
Pinch of Dry Thyme
Salt & Pepper to Taste
½ cup Pecorino Romano Cheese
¼ cup Fresh Flat Leaf Parsley (chopped)
½ cup White Wine
Pasta of Choice

1. Sauté garlic in olive oil until golden brown.
2. Add thyme, salt and pepper.
3. Add chic peas and wine. Cook for about 8 to 10 minutes. May need a little water.
4. Boil pasta Al Dante, drain and add to sauté above.
5. Toss together thoroughly adding parsley, breadcrumbs and cheese while tossing.

Serve Family Style

Lasagna

1 pound lean Ground Beef or Sirloin
1 pound Bulk Italian Sausage (hot or mild)
1 - 15 ounce tub Ricotta Cheese
16 ounces Shredded Mozzarella Cheese
1 pound Dry Lasagna Noodles
Parmesan Cheese
Marinara Sauce

1. Boil lasagna noodles until they are about half cooked, hard but somewhat bendable. Rinse and set aside.
2. Fry ground beef completely breaking it apart into small pieces with your spatula while cooking. Drain completely and dispose grease; set aside.
3. Fry sausage completely also breaking it apart into small pieces with your spatula while cooking. Drain and keep sausage drippings; set aside.
4. In a large bowl combine ricotta cheese, beef and sausage mixing them together thoroughly forming it into a meat and cheese paste.
5. In a large greased baking pan (13x9x2), set a layer of lasagna noodles covering entire bottom. Line them up in one direction going lengthwise in the pan.
6. Apply a generous layer of the meat and cheese paste over noodles.
7. Spoon out marinara sauce completely covering meat and cheese surface.
8. Sprinkle Mozzarella and parmesan cheese over sauce.
9. Go back to Step 6 and make 2 more layers.
10. Top the third layer with one more layer of noodles. This time coat noodles with sauce and top with mozzarella and parmesan cheese.
11. Wrap top with plastic wrap and then with tin foil. Bake at 350°F for 1 hour.

Let set up for 15 to 20 minutes before serving.

Baked Manicotti

PASTA
4 Large Eggs
1 cup Flour
¼ tsp Salt
1 cup Water
Vegetable Oil

Beat eggs slightly. Add salt and water, blend together. Slowly add flour and mix until smooth. Consistency should be a thin batter. Heat a griddle on medium temperature and grease with a light coating of oil. Cook as you would a pancake, making 4 to 6 inch circles. When finished set aside and let cool until needed.

NOTE: You can add flavoring to your dough by adding any chopped herb that you wish.

FILLING
2 pounds Ricotta Cheese
4 Large Eggs
¾ tsp Salt
½ cup Pecorino Romano or Parmesan Cheese (grated)
¼ tsp Ground Black Pepper
2 tbsp Fresh Flat Leaf Parsley (chopped)

Mix all ingredients in a large bowl. Spoon 1 to 2 tablespoons of the filling into the center of each dough circle, spreading it slightly and roll up. Place in a shallow baking pan and cover with marinara sauce and shredded mozzarella cheese. Bake at 375°F for 25 to 30 minutes. Serve immediately.

Stuffed Shells

1 box Jumbo Shell Pasta
½ pound Ground Beef
½ pound Loose Italian Sausage (hot or mild)
2 cloves Fresh Garlic (minced)
¼ cup Onion (chopped fine)
2 package Spinach (chopped and cooked)
2 Large Eggs
1 pound Ricotta Cheese
1 pound Mozzarella Cheese (shredded)
½ cup Pecorino Romano or Parmesan Cheese (grated)

1. Boil shell pasta until Al Dante. Set aside until needed.
2. Fry both ground beef and sausage separately, draining grease completely. Place in large bowl.
3. Sauté onions and garlic until onions are translucent. Add Spinach and cook until spinach shrinks down. Add to meat mix.
4. In a separate bowl, mix ricotta cheese and eggs until smooth. Add to meat and spinach mix. Blend well.
5. Slowly add shredded mozzarella and grated cheese while continuing to mix well.
6. Stuff each pasta shell and place in baking pan.
7. Cover shells with marinara sauce and bake for 30 minutes at 350°F.

Serve buffet style or plate individual topped with extra sauce and grated cheese if desired.

CLASSIC RECIPE

Use the filling from the Baked Manicotti recipe to stuff the shells with for a classic flavor.

Città di Bagnoregio

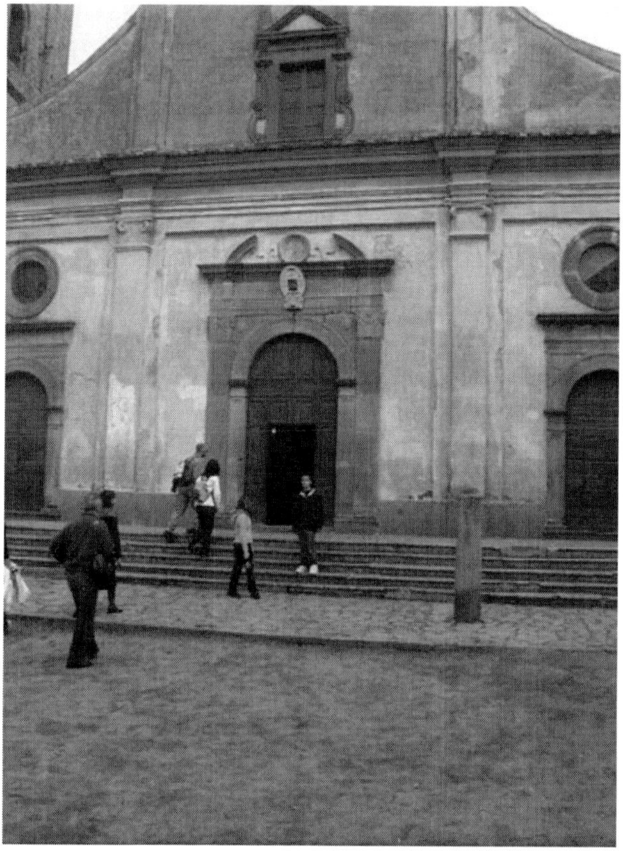

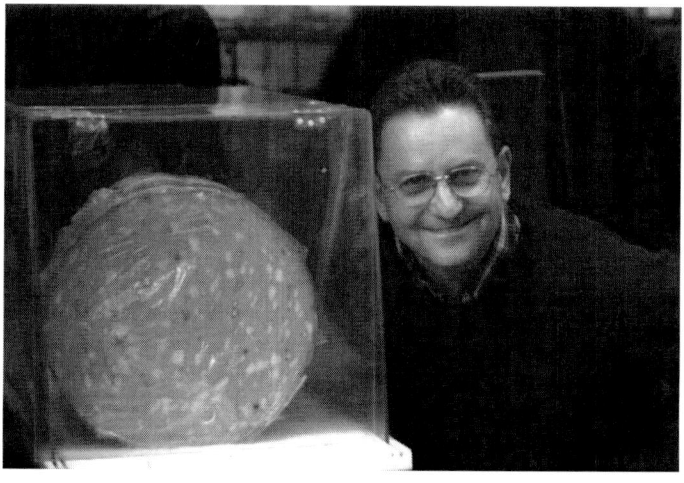

Land and Sea
(terra e mare)

Piccata

Piccata is traditionally made with veal, but can also be made with chicken scaloppini (cutlets).

4 Select Cutlets (pounded thin)
½ cup Flour
¼ tsp Salt
¼ tsp Pepper
6 tbsp Unsalted Butter (melted)
½ cup Chicken Stock
½ cup White Wine or Sherry
1 Lemon
1 tbsp Capers

1. Combine flour, salt and pepper in a shallow dish and generously coat cutlets.
2. In a hot sauté pan add butter and cook veal until done.
3. Add chicken stock, white wine, capers and squeeze entire lemon into pan.
4. Reduce heat and stir pan mixing all ingredients.
5. Serve by itself or over your favorite pasta (Angel Hair works best). Garnish with a lemon wheel dusted with paprika.

Marsala

> *Like Piccata, Marsala style is an Italian dish made from either veal or chicken scaloppini (cutlets).*

4 Select Cutlets (pounded thin)
½ cup Flour
¼ tsp Salt
¼ tsp Pepper
6 tbsp Unsalted Butter (melted)
½ cup Beef Stock
½ cup Sweet Marsala Wine
1 clove Fresh Garlic (minced)
4 ounces White Button Mushrooms (sliced)
1 tbsp Fresh Fresh Flat Leaf Parsely (chopped)

1. Combine flour, salt and pepper in a shallow dish and generously coat cutlets.
2. In a hot sauté pan add butter and garlic, cook chicken until done.
3. Add beef stock, Marsala wine and mushrooms. Continue to cook until mushrooms are soft.
4. Reduce heat and stir pan mixing all ingredients.
5. Add parsley just before serving.

Serve by itself or over your favorite pasta. Long flat pastas (linguini or fettuccini) seem to work better with this dish.

Parmesan

Almost anything can be cooked Parmesan style. Beside the favorite veal and chicken, you can also use a variety of seafood and fish.

4 Select Cutlets (pounded thin) or Seafood Selection
½ cup Flour
1 cup Bread Crumbs
2 Large Eggs
2 cups Marinara Sauce
4 ounces (1 ball) Fresh Mozzarella Cheese
2 ounces Parmesan Cheese (grated)

1. Flour cutlets. Egg dip, then coat generously with bread crumbs.
2. In a hot skillet, fry cutlets in vegetable oil until golden brown and done.
3. Remove cutlets from skillet and let sit on paper napkins to dry and drain excess oil.
4. Place cutlets on a baking pan and cover completely with Marinara sauce.
5. Slice mozzarella and top chicken and sauce. Sprinkle parmesan evenly.
6. Bake or broil in a hot oven until cheese melts over tops.

EGGPLANT PARMESAN

Fry sliced eggplant the way you fried the cutlets. In a greased deep baking (9"x13") layer eggplant, sauce and cheeses. Make 2 to 3 layers and bake at 350 °F for 30 to 45 minutes.

Cacciatore

Cacciatore means "hunter" in Italian. Cacciatore style refers to cooking hunter style with peppers, onions, mushrooms and tomatoes. Classically this dish is made with chicken or rabbit.

1 - 6 Piece Chicken (breasts, legs and thighs - skinless)
¼ cup Olive Oil
1 Large Onion (chopped medium)
1 Large Green Bell Pepper (cut into ¼ pieces)
2 cloves Fresh Garlic (minced)
6 Fresh Basil Leaves (chopped)
¼ cup Fresh Fresh Flat Leaf Parsely (chopped)
½ cup Red Table Wine
1 - 28oz. can Whole Peeled Tomatoes (hand crushed)
Salt & Pepper to Taste

1. In a large pot, brown chicken in olive oil.
2. When chicken is lightly browned on all sides add onion, pepper, garlic, basil and parsley. Continue cooking until chicken is golden brown and vegetables are softened.
3. Add wine, salt and pepper. Continue cooking until wine evaporates.
4. Add hand crushed tomatoes in their juices and let simmer for about 30 minutes until chicken is tender and sauce has thickened slightly.

Serve over rice or by itself in a bowl.

VARIATION

Try using equal parts medium diced chicken breast, veal, pork and sausage or try any wild meat such as deer, bear or rabbit.

Stuffed Peppers

10 - 12 Green or Red Bell Peppers
1 pound Meatball Mix (see recipe)
1 cup Cooked White Rice
Marinara Sauce
Grated Pecorino Romano Cheese

1. Slice tops off of peppers, emptying out seeds and centers.
2. Combine meatball mix and rice thoroughly and stuff each pepper slightly over tops, overfilling each pepper.
3. Place peppers in baking pan and generously top with marinara sauce.
4. Bake at 350°F for 30 minutes covered then 30 minutes uncovered. Sprinkle with Romano cheese and serve.

Baked Sausage & Peppers

2 Green Bell Peppers (gutted and sliced)
2 Red Bell Peppers (gutted and sliced)
2 Italian "Long Hot" Peppers (sliced)
1 large Onion (sliced)
2 cloves Garlic (minced)
2 pounds Italian Sausage (hot or mild)
2 Fresh Basil Leaves
Olive Oil

1. Place garlic, peppers, onions and sausage in baking pan. Drizzle with olive oil and top with Basil Leaves.
2. Bake at 350 °F for 1 to 1½ hours, stirring every 12 to 15 minutes.

Try adding sliced mushrooms for a variation.

Italian Meat Pie (Sausage Pie)

CRUST:
6 Large Eggs
2 tbsp Baking Soda
2½ cups Shortening
1 cup Milk
½ tsp Salt
Enough Flour to Form Dough (about 8 cups)

Cream together eggs and shortening. Add baking soda, milk and salt. Add flour 1 cup at a time until dough forms. Chill until ready to use.

FILLING:
2 pound Cooked Bulk Italian Sausage (hot or mild)
½ pound Chopped Ham
6 Hard Boiled Large Eggs
¾ cup Pecorino Romano or Parmesan Cheese
1 pound Fresh Mozzarella Cheese
1 pound Ricotta Cheese
1 tbsp Fresh Fresh Flat Leaf Parsely (chopped)
Salt to Taste

Mix all ingredients together in a large bowl.

METHOD:
1. Roll crust to fit the bottom of a cookie sheet.
2. Spread filling evenly over entire surface.
3. Roll out another crust to cover the top of the filling. Pinch edges closed.
4. Brush with egg wash and bake at 375°F until dough is cooked and brown, about 30 minutes.

Giambotta

I have found many varieties of this recipe, but in my eyes there is only one true Giambotta that tastes best after a night out on the town.

1 Green Bell Pepper (gutted and diced medium)
2 Hot Cherry Peppers (gutted and diced medium)
1 large Onion (medium chopped)
½ pound Pre-cooked Italian Sausage Links (hot or mild)
2 Large Potatoes (cut bite size)
4 Large Eggs
4 ounces Mozzarella (shredded)
1 cup Escarole (washed and blanched)

1. Cut potatoes into small bite size pieces and boil until firm but done.
2. Cut up all your vegetables and sauté in olive oil until tender.
3. Cut the sausage into small ½ inch slices and add to vegetables. Continue cooking for about 2 to 3 minutes tossing everything in the skillet around.
4. Add potatoes into the skillet. Continue cooking for another 2 to 3 minutes once again tossing everything in the skillet around.
5. Add Escarole and continue sautéing for another minute.
6. Make a hole in the center of the mix, pushing the cooked vegetable to the sides of the skillet.
7. Pour eggs into skillet center and scramble separately from vegetables. When eggs are fully cooked, incorporate them into the vegetable mix.
8. Just before serving, toss in shredded mozzarella cheese and lightly fold into mix.

Serve with a side of Marinara Sauce or just drizzle over top.

Stuffed Calamari

3 pounds Squid Bodies (cleaned)
6 Hard Boiled Large Eggs
1 cup Italian Style Bread Crumbs
1 clove Fresh Garlic (minced)
1 tsp Fresh Fresh Flat Leaf Parsely (chopped)
¼ tsp Fresh Basil (chopped)
3 tbsp Pecorino Romano or Parmesan Cheese (grated)
Salt and Fresh Ground Pepper to Taste

1. Chop eggs fine and mix in garlic, parsley, basil, salt, pepper and cheese.
2. Mix in bread crumbs.
3. Stuff squid and close openings with wet toothpicks.
4. Fry gently in vegetable oil then drop into marinara sauce. (you can also put in sauce without frying)

Shrimp Scampi

1 pound Large Shrimp (peeled & deveined)
2 cloves Fresh Garlic (minced)
½ stick Butter
1 Lemon
White Wine or Sherry
Fresh Fresh Flat Leaf Parsely (chopped)

1. In a hot skillet, sauté shrimp and garlic in butter.
2. Tossing shrimp around in the skillet until all sides have turned white.
3. Squeeze a whole lemon into sauté, then add wine.
4. Allow wine to cook off for a couple minutes then toss in the parsley.

Serve by itself, over rice or pasta.

Firenze

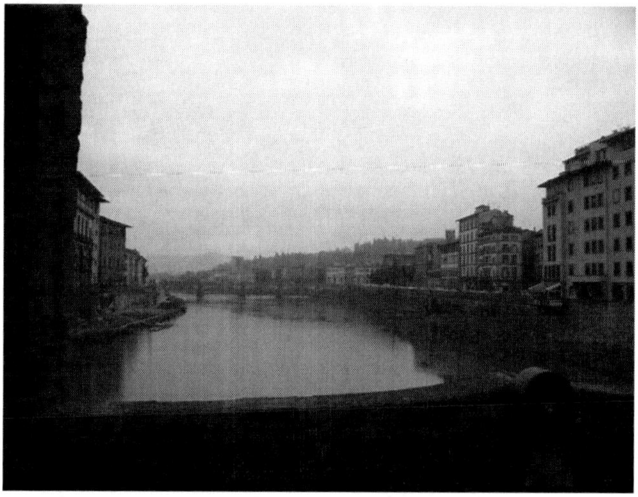

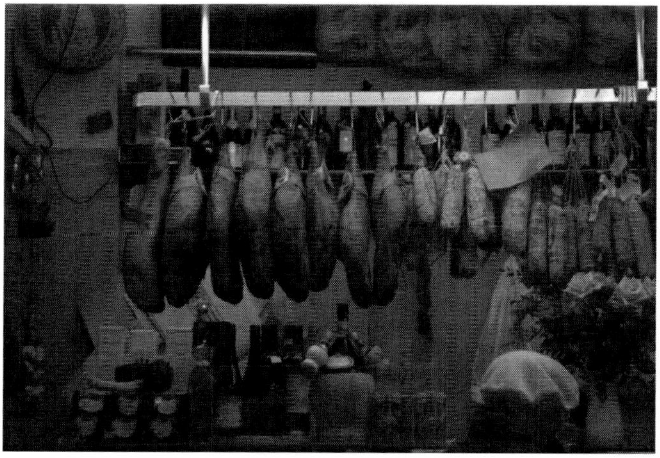

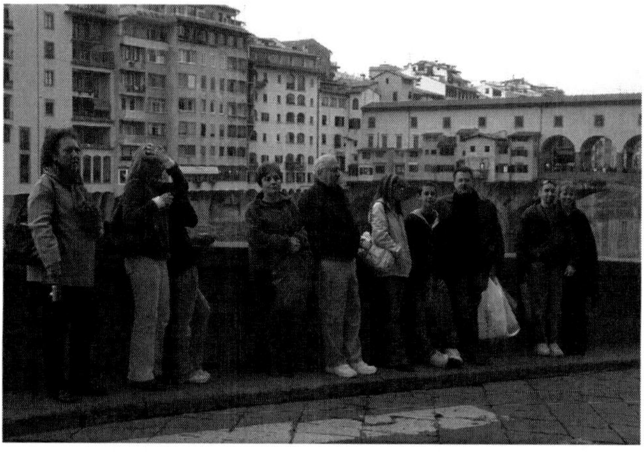

Desserts
(dolce)

Chocolate Pustichioti (Pusties)

Dough
1½ cups Lard or Shortening
6 cups Flour
1¼ cups Brown Sugar
3 Large Eggs (1 for wash)
½ cup Cold Water
½ tsp Baking Powder
¼ cup Honey

Filling
½ cup Flour
1 cup Sugar
¼ cup Cocoa Powder
1 cup Whole Milk
1 cup Cold Water

1. Blend together shortening and sugar. Add water, honey and 2 eggs continuing to blend.
2. Add baking powder then flour and knead like you would a pie crust. Add a little more flour if dough is too soft. Knead and refrigerate.
3. Mix together in a small bowl flour, sugar and cocoa. Set aside.
4. In a small pot mix milk and water. Add flour/sugar/cocoa mixture and stir over medium heat until thickened. Remove from heat when thick.
5. Roll the dough into meatball size balls and spread into greased Pustie tins (use non-stick Brioche tins if you can find them).
6. Fill each tin with filling, leaving room for a top.
7. Roll remaining dough and cut circular tops for the tins. Cover each tin with a top and pinch outer edges closed.
8. Brush tops with egg wash and bake in a preheated oven at 375 °F for 20 to 25 minutes.

Vanilla Pustichioti (Pusties)

Dough
1½ cups Lard or Shortening
6 cups Flour
1¼ cups Brown Sugar
3 Large Eggs (1 for wash)
½ cup Cold Water
½ tsp Baking Powder
¼ cup Honey

Filling
3 Large Eggs
¾ cup Sugar
½ cup Flour
2 cups Whole Milk
1 tsp Vanilla Extract
Dab of Butter

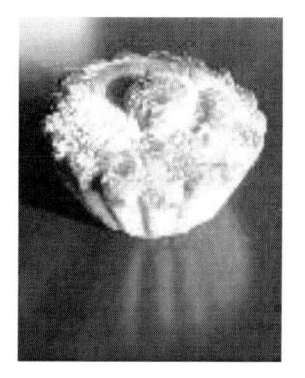

1. Blend together shortening and sugar. Add water, honey and 2 eggs continuing to blend.
2. Add baking powder then flour and knead like you would a pie crust. Add a little more flour if dough is too soft. Knead and refrigerate.
3. Mix together flour, sugar and cocoa in a small bowl. Set aside.
4. In a small pot mix filling ingredients and stir over medium heat until thickened. Remove from heat when thick.
5. Roll the dough into meatball size balls and spread into greased Pustie tins (use non-stick Brioche tins if you can find them).
6. Fill each tin with filling, leaving room for a top.
7. Roll remaining dough and cut circular tops for the tins. Cover each tin with a top and pinch outer edges closed. Pinch off a small piece of dough and place it on each Pustie. This will mark the difference between the chocolate and vanilla Pusties.
8. Brush tops with egg wash and bake in a preheated oven at 375 °F for 20 to 25 minutes.

Hemstrought's Half Moon Cookies

This cake-like cookie is unique to Utica, New York. It is believed to be originated by Hemstrought's Bakery.

COOKIES:
3¾ cups Flour
¾ tsp Baking Powder
2 tsp Baking Soda
2¼ cups Sugar
16 tbsp Margarine (2 sticks)
¾ cup Cocoa Powder
¼ tsp Salt
2 Large Eggs
1 tsp Vanilla Extract
1½ cups Milk

Preheat oven to 350°F. Line cookie sheets with parchment paper. Sift together flour, baking powder, and baking soda in a medium bowl and set aside. Put sugar, margarine, cocoa, and salt in bowl and beat on medium speed until fluffy. Add eggs and vanilla and continue to beat. Add half the milk, then half the flour mixture, beating after each addition until smooth; repeat with remaining milk and flour mixture. Spoon or pipe batter onto parchment-lined baking sheets, making 3" rounds 2 inches apart.

Bake until cookies are set, about 12 to 15 minutes. Allow to cool, then remove from parchment.

Continued on next page . . .

FUDGE ICING:
3½ oz Bittersweet Chocolate
3½ oz Semisweet Chocolate
1 tbsp Butter
4¼ cups Confectioners Sugar
2 tbsp Corn Syrup
1 tsp Vanilla Extract
Pinch salt

Melt bittersweet and semisweet chocolates with butter in a double boiler. Add confectioners sugar, corn syrup, vanilla, salt and 6 tablespoons of boiling water, mix to a smooth stiff paste with a rubber spatula. Thin icing with up to 6 more tablespoons of boiling water. Icing should fall from a spoon in thick ribbons. Keep icing warm in a double boiler over low heat.

BUTTER CREAM ICING:
7 cups Confectioners Sugar
16 tbsp Unsalted Butter (softened, cut into pieces)
½ cup Vegetable Shortening
7 tbsp Milk
1 tbsp Vanilla Extract
Pinch salt

Put sugar, butter, shortening, milk, vanilla, and salt in the bowl of a standing mixer. Beat on low speed to mix, then increase to medium and beat until light and fluffy.

FROSTING THE COOKIES:
Let the cookies set for about an hour in your refrigerator before icing. Using a metal spatula, spread about 1 teaspoon of warm fudge icing on half of the flat side of each cookie. Spread the other half of each cookie with 1 heaping teaspoon butter cream icing.

Black and White Cookies

COOKIES:
1 cup Unsalted Butter (softened)
1¾ cups Sugar
4 each Eggs
1 cup Milk
½ tsp Vanilla Extract
¼ tsp Lemon Extract
5 cups Flour
1 tsp Baking Powder
½ tsp Salt

Preheat oven to 350°F. Line cookie sheets with parchment paper. Mix together flour, baking powder, and salt in a medium bowl and set aside. Cream sugar, butter, vanilla, and lemon extract in bowl on medium speed until fluffy. Add eggs one at a time while continuing to beat. Add milk, then slowly add flour mixture, beat until smooth. Spoon or pipe batter onto parchment-lined baking sheets, making 3" rounds 2 inches apart. Bake until cookies are set, about 15 to 20 minutes. Allow to cool, then remove from parchment.

FROSTING:
4 cups Confectioners Sugar
¼ cup Boiling Water
1 oz. Bittersweet Chocolate (chopped)

Place confectioners sugar in large bowl. Mix in boiling water one tablespoon at a time until mixture is thick and spreadable. Transfer half of the frosting to the top of a double boiler set over simmering water. Stir in the chocolate until chocolate melts. Remove from heat.

With a brush, coat half the cookie with chocolate frosting and the other half with the white frosting. Set on waxed paper until frosting hardens.

Grandma's Cookies

DOUGH:
7 cups Flour
6 Large Eggs
6 tsp Baking Powder
1 ½ cup Sugar
1 cup Vegetable Oil
1 cup Water
1 tbsp Vanilla Extract

FROSTING:
Confectioners Sugar
Non-Perils
Water

1. Mix all dough ingredients together in large bowl.
2. Roll dough into half inch ropes. Cut each rope into 4 inch segments and tie in a knot.
3. Place them on a greased cookie sheet about 1 inch apart and cook for about 10 minutes at 350 °F or until slightly brown.
4. Let cool completely before frosting. Top with non-perils.

Date Nut Cookies

DOUGH:
2½ cups Shortening
4 Large Egg Yolks
1 cup Sugar
1 cup Orange Juice
1½ tsp Vanilla Extract
6 cups Flour
1 tsp Baking Soda
1 tsp Baking Powder
½ tsp Salt

Beat together shortening, egg yolks, sugar and vanilla. Mix all dry ingredients together and blend into wet mix. Slowly add orange juice while kneading dough. Add more flour if sticky.

FILLING:
1 pound Minced Dates
1 cup Chopped Nuts (your choice)
¼ cup Water
¼ cup Brown Sugar
1 jar Peach Jam

Combine all ingredients (except nuts) in a medium sauce pan and cook until sugar dissolves. Add nuts and remove from stove.

METHOD:
Roll dough out and cut with round glass. Place a tablespoon of filling in the center of each round and roll up. Cook at 375°F for 15 minutes.

Biscotti

½ cup Butter (softened)
1 - 4 oz. package Cream Cheese
1 cup Sugar
4 Large Eggs
3½ cups Flour
3 tsp Baking Powder
1 tsp Anise Extract
1 cup Slivered Almonds
Pinch of Salt

1. Blend butter and cream cheese together.
2. Gradually add sugar while continuing to blend.
3. Beat in eggs one at a time.
4. Continue to beat until light and fluffy.
5. Mix all dry ingredients in a separate bowl and slowly add them to the beaten mix.
6. Knead into a dough, slowly adding whole almonds as you knead. Add more flour if dough is too sticky.
7. Shape into oval rolls about 1½ to 2 inches thick.
8. Bake at 350°F for 30 minutes.
9. Let cool slightly and splice into 1 inch slices.
10. Lay each piece on it's side and toast for 10 to 15 minutes on each side in a 375°F oven.

VARIATIONS

To add flavor to your Biscotti, try using different extracts and different nuts.

Also try dipping half of each biscotti in melted chocolate and let cool to harden.

Pita en Cue (Christmas Pie)

CRUST:
4½ cups Flour
4 Large Eggs
1 cup Sugar
1 cup Butter (softened)
½ cup Milk

Cream together sugar and butter. Add eggs and beat well. Add milk and flour and knead into a dough. Chill until ready to use.

FILLING:
3 jar Honey
4 boxes Raisins
4 - 8oz packs Walnuts (chopped)
1 - 8oz. pack Almonds (sliced)
Cinnamon

METHOD:
1. Roll out enough dough to form a bottom in a square cake pan (suggested 8"x8"x2").
2. Roll remainder of the dough out long and oblong.
3. Spread honey over entire dough.
4. Next sprinkle the dough with the following in order: Cinnamon, chopped walnuts and raisins.
5. Roll the dough into a spiral long way and cut into pieces the thickness of the cake pan.
6. Put each roll into the cake pan with the spiral end up, filling the entire pan.
7. Sprinkle top with almond slices, raisins and walnuts to fill in any spaces.
8. Bake at 350ºF for 1 hour until brown.
9. When removed from oven immediately drizzle honey over top.

Pinulattas (Honey Balls)

> *This Sicilian recipe goes way back to the great grandparents that came to America many years ago. These are also called Struffella or Struffoli, depending on what part of Italy your family roots can be traced to. In my family, we traditionally made these at Christmas time.*

6 Large Eggs
¼ cup Vegetable Oil
½ tsp Baking Powder
3 cups Flour
1 cup Honey w/ 1 tbsp Sugar
Almond Slivers
Non-Perils

1. Beat eggs and oil until smooth.
2. Mix baking powder into flour and add to egg mix.
3. Knead into dough. Add more flour if dough is too sticky.
4. Roll dough out into long ½ inch ropes. Cut each rope into ½ inch pieces. Set aside.
5. In a deep fryer or deep frying pan, fry little dough balls until golden brown (about 1 minute).
6. Remove balls and drain them on paper towels.
7. Once all the dough is fried, pile them in pie tins about 2 inches high. Boil honey and sugar together, then drizzle generously over dough balls and finish by sprinkling almond slivers non-perils.

Pizzelles

½ cup Salted Butter (1 stick)
3 Large Eggs
¾ cup Sugar
1¾ cup Flour
2 tsp Vanilla or Anise Extract
1 tsp Baking Powder
Confectioners Sugar

1. Cream butter, sugar, eggs and extract together until smooth.
2. Mix in baking powder and flour.
3. Spoon onto a hot Pizzelle iron and cook for 1 minute.
4. Finish by sprinkling with confectioners sugar.

ADDING FLAVOR TO YOUR PIZZELLS

- Substitute other flavored extracts for Anise.
- Substitute ground spices for extract. Try cinnamon, nutmeg and allspice equally to a 2 teaspoon measurement.
- Replace ¼ cup of flour with ¼ cup of cocoa powder or ground semisweet chocolate.
- Immediately after you take the Pizzelle out of the iron, fold it over like a taco shell and fill with your favorite pie filling or fresh fruit.
- Substitute 1 packet of your favorite pudding mix for extract. You may need to a little bit of water if dough is too stiff.
- Try grinding your favorite nuts fine and add them to your mix. Make sure you stay within your flavor scheme.

Tiramisu

3 Large Eggs (separated)
1 pound Mascarpone or Ricotta Cheese
1 Orange (to zest)
¼ cup Sugar
2 packages Lady Fingers
1½ cups Strong Espresso Coffee
Cocoa Powder

1. Beat egg yolks and sugar well until smooth and creamy. Add cheese and beat for 2 to 3 more minutes. Fold in orange zest.
2. Beat egg whites to stiff peaks (meringue consistency).
3. Layer lady fingers in bottom of cake pan. Drizzle espresso over layer.
4. Spread cheese mixture evenly on top of lady fingers.
5. With a shaker, cover entire cheese mixture layer with a fair amount of cocoa powder.
6. Repeat from Step 3 making two layers.

Chill for at least 1 hour before serving.

VARIATIONS

- After spreading the cheese layer, press in fresh strawberries into cheese mixture.
- Add grated chocolate into the cheese mix in Step 1 for a Chocolate Lovers Tiramisu.
- Mix in your favorite flavored liqueur into espresso before drizzling.

Italian Sponge Cake

8 Large Eggs (separate whites and yolks)
2 tsp Grated Lemon Rind
2 tsp Almond Extract
1¼ cups Cake Flour
1¼ cups Sugar
1½ tbsp Water
¼ tsp Salt

1. Mix ½ cup sugar with the flour.
2. Place egg yolks, water and grated lemon rind in a bowl and beat lightly. Add almond extract.
3. Sift flour lightly over beaten egg yolks and fold in gently.
4. Place egg whites in another bowl and beat until foamy. Add salt and remainder of the sugar. Beat until stiff.
5. Gently fold the egg whites into the flour mixture. Pour into baking dish. Bake 45 minutes until cake separates from sides of pan.

Leave in pan 1 hour until cold.

Zabaglione (Marsala Custard)

8 Large Egg Yolks
¼ cup Sugar
1 cup Marsala Wine
2 tbsp Brandy
1 tbsp Water

1. Place egg yolks in sugar in the top part of a double boiler. Beat well with wire whisk.
2. Add wine and brandy continuing to beat well.
3. Add water continuing to beat well.
4. Place the pan over hot water, beat or stir until mixture thickens. DO NOT LET IT BOIL.

Italian Rum Cake

1 recipe Italian Sponge Cake (refer to recipe)
1 recipe Zabaglione (refer to recipe)
Chocolate pudding, cooled
1 quart Sliced Strawberries
Whipped Cream
Toasted Slivered Almonds
Rum or Rum with syrup water

1. Slice the sponge cake horizontally into at least three layers.
2. Drizzle the rum or rum syrup mixture over the bottom layer until fairly moist but not soaked.
3. Spread Zabaglione over entire layer.
4. Place sliced strawberries evenly over the Zabaglione.
5. Place the middle cake layer over the strawberries Drizzle the cake layer with more rum or rum syrup mixture until fairly moist but not soaked.
6. Spread this layer with chocolate pudding.
7. Place Top layer of cake over the chocolate pudding.
8. Drizzle with more rum or rum syrup mixture.
9. Cover cake with whipped cream. Push sliced almonds into sides of cake.

Let the cake sit for at least 4 hours in the refrigerator until rum saturates and chilled.

Cassata (Easter Pie)

CRUST:
4 Large Eggs
1 cup Sugar
1 cup Butter
½ cup Milk
3 - 4 cups Flour

Beat together eggs and sugar. Add butter and milk and continue beating another minute. Add mix with flour, kneading into a pie crust consistency. Add more flour if too sticky. Once dough is ready refrigerate for 1 hour before using.

FILLING:
2 dozen Large Eggs
2 pounds Ricotta Cheese
1 ½ Large Hershey Chocolate Bar (grated)
3 cups Sugar
1 tbsp Cinnamon
2 ounces Citron (diced) - *optional*

With a mixer, beat eggs for about 15 to 20 minutes until frothy and smooth. While eggs are beating, in another bowl mix Ricotta, sugar, grated chocolate, and cinnamon. Mix until smooth and creamy. Add Citron last.
Once eggs are beaten, combine them with the cheese mixture and whisk well.

PUTTING TOGETHER
Roll dough out into a large circle. Transfer dough into a 12 inch spring pan, covering all sides and overlapping outer edges. Pour Filling into dough pan and bake for 3 hours at 325ºF. DO NOT OPEN OVEN WHILE COOKING OR JUMP UP AND DOWN NEAR THE OVEN. THE CASSATA WILL FALL IF NOT CAREULL!!!!!
Cool at room temperature for 1 hour, then transfer to refrigerator and let cool overnight before eating.

Gelato (Italian Ice Cream)

5 Large Eggs
1 cup Sugar
2 cups Crushed Flavored Cookies of Your Choice
    (this is what gives the Gelato it's flavoring)
2 cups Heavy Whipping Cream
1 ounce Vanilla Extract or ½ ounce of Rum

1. Separate egg yolks from egg whites, keeping them both.
2. Beat egg yolks slowly adding sugar until smooth.
3. Add extract (or rum) and whipping cream. Continue to beat until mix doubles in size.
4. Add cookies and mix at a slower speed, making sure crushed cookies are thoroughly blended into cream.
5. Whip egg whites until a firm meringue texture and fold into mixture.
6. Pour into a storage container and freeze.

FLAVOR SUGGESTIONS

Since the Gelato takes on the flavor of the cookies used, try using some unique flavors each time you make this Italian Ice Cream favorite.

Mint Oreos ❋ Amaretto Biscotti ❋ Chocolate Chip
Fig Newtons ❋ Peanut Butter ❋ Butter Pecan
White Chocolate Chip Macadamia Nut
Oatmeal Raisin ❋ Snickerdoodle

Pizza Fritte

This fried dough recipe has been around for decades and can actually be eaten as a breakfast pastry or as a dessert with any meal.

6 cups Flour
1 package Dry Yeast
1 ¾ cups Water
Granulated Sugar
Frying Oil

1. Mix flour and 2 teaspoons of salt together in a bowl. Dissolve yeast in 1 cup of warm water and add to flour mix. Add remaining water and knead dough for about 20 minutes. Add extra flour if sticky. Place in an oiled bowl and cover with dry towel. Set aside in a warm place and let rise.
2. Heat frying oil in a deep pan until hot enough to deep fry with (280°C).
3. Once dough has doubled in size, knead for another 10 minutes and spread onto baking sheet. Set aside and cover with towel to rise again.
4. Pinch off large pieces of dough from the risen dough ball and shape into flat discs about four inches in diameter.
5. Fry dough pieces on both sides for about a minute per side.
6. Remove fried dough and place on paper towels to drain. Immediately sprinkle sugar over both sides when hot.

Best served hot within minutes of cooking.

Your Personal Recipes

Recipe _____

Recipe

Recipe _____

Recipe _____

Recipe

Recipe _____

Recipe _____

Recipe

Recipe _____

Recipe

Made in United States
North Haven, CT
21 November 2023